good answers
to tough questions

About Substance Abuse

Written by Joy Berry

CHILDRENS PRESS ®

CHICAGO

Managing Editor: Lana Eberhard
Copy Editors: Annette Gooch, Judy Lockwood
Contributing Editors: John Bilitch, Ph.D.,
Libby Byers, Ilene Frommer, James Gough, M.D.,
Dan Gurney, Charles Pengra, Ph.D.
Contributing Physician: James S. Gough, M.D.

Art Direction: Communication Graphics
Designer: Jennifer Wiezel
Illustration Designer: Bartholomew
Inking Artist: Alyson Butler
Lettering Artist: Linda Hanney
Coloring Artist: Teri Jones
Typography and Production: Communication Graphics

Published by Childrens Press
in cooperation with Living Skills Press

This book presents information about the following:
- Important terms you should know
- Nonprescription and prescription drugs
- Why you might be tempted to abuse drugs
- Why you should *not* abuse drugs
- How you can avoid drug abuse
- How you can say *no* to drug use

Look around and you'll see a lot of different things in your environment.

These things are neither good nor bad in and of themselves. It's how you use them that makes them good or bad.

There are two ways to use things. When you use things in a **positive** way, you make life better for yourself and other people.

When you use things in a **negative** way, (**abuse** them), you harm yourself and other people.

Drugs are substances in your environment that are neither good nor bad in and of themselves. It is how you use them that makes them good or bad.

Using drugs in a positive way — using them to improve your health and well-being — can make life better for yourself and for other people.

Using drugs in a negative way — abusing them — can destroy your health and well-being. Drug abuse harms you and harms other people.

Abusing drugs can cause you to become **physically addicted** to or **psychologically dependent** on them.

- When you become physically addicted to a drug, your body becomes dependent on it and cannot function normally without it.
- When you become psychologically dependent on a drug, you believe that you cannot function without it and so you feel compelled to use it.

Overcoming drug addiction or dependence is difficult and painful.

Some people use drugs as a form of recreation. Using drugs in this way is abusing them.

You must decide for yourself whether to use drugs for recreation. However, before you make this decision, you need to know some facts about drugs, including the reasons people use them and the effects drug abuse can have.

Alcohol is a drug found in beer, wine, and liquor.

Some people drink alcohol to help themselves relax and feel more at ease. Others use it to make themselves feel outgoing or daring.

Before you decide that drinking might be a good way to relax, consider some of the effects of alcohol abuse:

- physical addiction,

- brain damage and serious problems in other organs,

- appetite disturbances,

- lack of energy and motivation,

- loss of balance and poor coordination,

- inability to think clearly and react quickly, and

- moodiness.

Drinking coffee or taking a cold shower cannot make you sober after drinking alcohol. Only the passing of time can make the effects wear off.

Marijuana is often called "dope" or "pot." This drug is also known as "grass" or "weed" because it comes from the dried stems, flowers, and leaves of certain plants.

Some people smoke or eat marijuana to help themselves relax. They also like the "high" (the sense of excitement and well-being) that the drug can produce.

People who tell you that "getting high" on marijuana won't hurt you probably won't tell you that marijuana abuse causes

- psychological dependency;

- damage to the nose, throat, and lungs;

- increased risk of infections;

- uncontrollable cravings for sweet foods;

- lack of energy or motivation;

- inability to think clearly and react quickly; and

- moodiness.

Beginning users of the drug often experience panic attacks and feel suspicious and unreasonably fearful.

Cocaine ("coke" or "crack") is a drug made from the leaves of the coca plant.

People who sniff, smoke, or inject cocaine say that the drug makes them feel confident, powerful, and energetic. Users also like the "rush" (an intense feeling of well-being) that cocaine gives them.

Some people will tell you that the "rush" you experience from cocaine is the most intense sensation you can get from any drug. But they probably won't tell you that this sensation is absolutely not worth the price you have to pay for it.

Cocaine is extremely addictive! Here are just a few of the other effects of cocaine abuse:

• risk of sudden death;

• high blood pressure and heart problems;

• increased risk of nose, throat, and lung infections;

• appetite disturbances and possible malnutrition;

• trouble falling asleep;

• hallucinations; and

• extreme changes in mood.

People who are withdrawing from cocaine often become seriously depressed. They also usually lack energy and motivation.

Hallucinogens are drugs that can produce intense mental, physical, and emotional reactions. Drugs such as LSD ("acid"), PCP ("angel dust"), MDA ("Ecstasy"), STP, and also certain desert plants such as peyote are hallucinogens.

People who use hallucinogens say that they like the intensely pleasurable experiences ("trips") these drugs can produce. Users believe that these "trips" bring them a powerful sense of increased awareness and understanding.

Like the cocaine "rush," the "trips" hallucinogens offer are never worth the price you have to pay for them. Here's why: hallucinogen abuse causes

- "bad trips" (terrifying mental and emotional experiences which can lead to long term emotional problems or even suicide),

- nausea and vomiting,

- severe panic attacks, and

- "flashbacks" ("bad trips" that occur without taking more of these drugs).

PCP use often causes people to become aggressive and physically violent and to take risks that can result in serious injuries or death.

Some people use certain kinds of **glues, liquid cleaners,** and **other chemical products** as drugs.

Users say that inhaling these drugs causes pleasant, light-headed, giddy feelings. Some people feel more outgoing and daring after sniffing these drugs.

You might think that glues and other chemical products aren't dangerous because they're household items that can be purchased by anyone almost anywhere. However, these products are considered by some doctors to be the most physically damaging substances used as drugs. Thus, you need to read the warnings on the labels and take them seriously.

Abusing these substances can cause

- death,

- brain damage and serious problems in other organs,

- nausea and vomiting, and

- loss of sensory perceptions (damage to the senses of sight, hearing, smell, taste, and touch).

Stimulants include diet pills and other kinds of "uppers." These drugs are also known as "speed," "bennies," and "white crosses."

Users say that these drugs help them feel more alert and reduce the need for sleep. People who want to lose weight sometimes use these drugs to help control their appetite.

Even though many stimulants are available in grocery and drug stores, these drugs can be extremely unsafe if they are abused.

They can cause

- psychological dependence,

- blood pressure and heart problems,

- uncontrolled weight loss and malnutrition,

- nervousness and restlessness,

- trouble falling asleep, and

- irritable feelings and extreme changes in mood.

People who are withdrawing from these drugs often become seriously depressed. They may also lack energy and motivation.

Sedatives include sleeping pills and other drugs known as "downers."

Some people use sedatives to feel drowsy so they can fall asleep easily. Other users simply like the relaxed feeling these drugs produce.

Just because doctors sometimes prescribe sedatives does not mean that these drugs are safe for you to take on your own. If you use sedatives without being told to do so by a doctor, you are putting yourself at risk because these drugs have some extremely harmful effects:

- high risk of death from overdose (especially when taken with alcohol or other drugs);

- physical addiction;

- increased risk of nose, throat, and lung infections;

- unwanted drowsiness;

- sleep disturbances;

- lack of energy and motivation; and

- inability to think clearly and react clearly.

Kids who use sedatives sometimes become extremely excitable.

People who are withdrawing from these drugs often feel nervous, restless, and irritable.

Tranquilizers are drugs that doctors sometimes prescribe to relieve tension and to relax painful muscles.

Some people use tranquilizers to help themselves feel more at ease.

Like sedatives, tranquilizers can be harmful if you take them without being told to do so by a doctor. They can cause

- death from overdose (especially when taken with alcohol or other drugs),

- physical addiction and psychological dependency,

- blurred vision,

- loss of balance and poor coordination,

- sleep disturbances,

- lack of energy, and

- irritable, hostile feelings.

Kids who use tranquilizers sometimes become extremely excitable.

Opiates are a type of "pain-killer." Although doctors sometimes prescribe certain opiates for pain relief, not all of these drugs are prescription drugs. Some, such as heroin, are illegal.

Some people use opiates because they like the drowsy, relaxed feelings these drugs can produce.

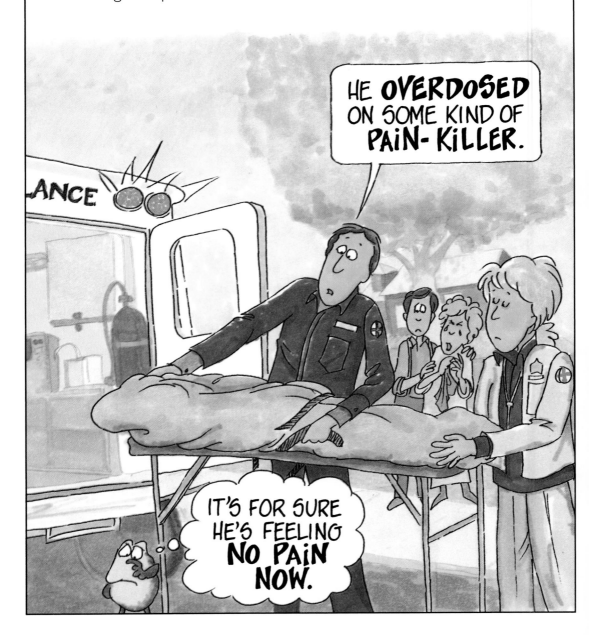

First-time users of opiates almost always become violently ill. From that point on, things usually go from bad to worse. Here's why: Abusing opiates causes such harmful effects as

- risk of sudden death,

- physical addiction,

- increased risk of infections,

- uncontrolled weight loss and possible malnutrition,

- exhaustion,

- severe loss of motivation, and

- depression.

People who are withdrawing from opiates often feel extremely irritable and physically uncomfortable.

Even though there is not one *good* reason for you ever to abuse drugs, there are a lot of reasons you might consider taking the risks, regardless of the danger.

You might be tempted to abuse drugs because of peer pressure.

Kids who abuse drugs often worry that their drug use will cause something bad to happen to them. They don't want to be alone in this dangerous situation, so they try to pressure other kids to take drugs, too.

You might be tempted to abuse drugs because they make you feel
- older,
- more mature, and
- more socially acceptable.

You might be tempted to abuse drugs because they make you feel
- stronger,
- more powerful,
- invincible,
- daring, or
- outgoing.

You might be tempted to abuse drugs because you are curious or bored and think that using drugs for recreation will be fun or exciting.

You might be tempted to abuse drugs to escape from the pressure you feel from expectations other people place upon you.

You might be tempted to abuse drugs to avoid facing and dealing with
- uncomfortable feelings,
- failure,
- problems,
- difficult situations, and
- trauma.

There is never a good reason to abuse drugs. However, there are plenty of good reasons for you *not* to abuse drugs.

You should not abuse drugs because drug abuse can cause severe damage to your brain, heart, lungs, liver, kidneys, and other parts of your body.

You should avoid drug abuse because the brain damage it can cause affects your sense of balance and coordination. This can increase the risk of your having a serious or fatal accident.

The damage to your brain can also make it difficult for you to think clearly and make good decisions.

You should not abuse drugs because drug abuse can encourage you to avoid facing your problems instead of resolving them. And not dealing properly with your problems can make your life unhappy and unproductive.

You should avoid drug abuse because it can take away your motivation to find better ways to have fun and relax. Using drugs for recreation can cause you to miss out on many of the wonderful experiences life has to offer.

You should not abuse drugs because you are more likely to become dependent on drugs and addicted to them if you begin using them at a young age.

You should not abuse drugs because it is against the law.

Drug abuse can also influence you to break the law in other ways.

Because drugs are often expensive, you might decide to do unlawful things to get the money to pay for them.

Even though avoiding drug abuse is the *smart* thing to do, it isn't always easy. You can make things much easier for yourself by following the recommendations on the next few pages.

Before you put any substance into your body, be certain that you know exactly what it is and what effect it will have on you.

Try to choose friends who do not abuse drugs.

Try to avoid situations that encourage drug abuse.

Keep a realistic perspective on life. Remember that the things you see in movies and advertisements do not always represent real life and that the information presented is not always accurate or true.

Be aware of and avoid doing things that make you appear to support drug abuse. Avoid the kinds of music, clothing, posters, mugs, and other items that feature alcohol or drug products that may encourage drug abuse.

Here are some things you can say when you are offered a drug:
- No thanks. I don't want it.
- No thanks. I don't like it.
- No thanks. I don't need it.
- No thanks. It makes me sick.
- No thanks. My parents told me that if I ever used drugs, they would punish me, and they mean it.
- No thanks. It's against the law and I don't want to risk getting myself or my friends into serious trouble.
- No thanks. If I used drugs it would disappoint a lot of people who believe in me.
- No thanks. It would ruin the reputation that I've worked to establish for myself.

Saying no is most effective when you walk away immediately after you have said it.

Walking away is your best defense against being talked into using drugs.

It is easier to say no to a person who offers you drugs when you are with friends who also want to say no.

Ask for support or help from friends or an adult if someone who has offered you drugs continues to pressure you after you have clearly said no.

Ask your parents or an older friend who can drive to pick you up and take you home if you are in a situation where there is overwhelming pressure to abuse drugs.

Remember, no one ever plans to become an alcoholic or drug addict.

Every alcoholic or drug addict once thought that he or she would never become addicted or dependent. *Everyone* who uses drugs risks becoming addicted or dependent on them.

The best way to avoid drug addiction and dependence is to avoid drug abuse.

No one can force you to abuse drugs. No one can keep you from abusing drugs.

The decision to avoid drug abuse is one that you must make for yourself.